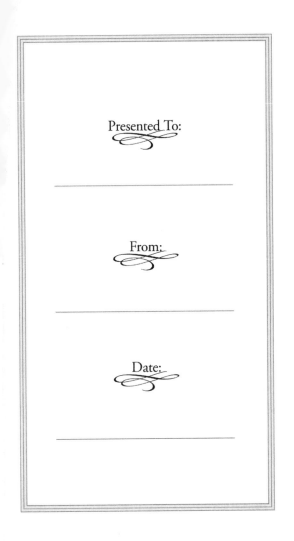

Presented To:

_____

From:

_____

Date:

_____

DISCOVERING Joye

DESTINY IMAGE BOOKS
BY JIM STOVALL

The Lamp

A Christmas Snow

DISCOVERING Joye

Uncovering the Treasures Inside Ordinary
People, Places, Things and Ourselves

JIM STOVALL

DESTINY IMAGE® PUBLISHERS, INC.
P.O. Box 310, Shippensburg, PA 17257-0310
"Promoting Inspired Lives."

This book and all other Destiny Image, Revival Press, MercyPlace, Fresh Bread, Destiny Image Fiction, and Treasure House books are available at Christian bookstores and distributors worldwide.

For a U.S. bookstore nearest you, call 1-800-722-6774. For more information on foreign distributors, call 717-532-3040.

Reach us on the Internet: www.destinyimage.com.

ISBN 13 TP: 978-0-7684-0354-1
ISBN 13 Ebook: 978-0-7684-8484-7

For Worldwide Distribution, Printed in Canada
1 2 3 4 5 6 7 8 / 17 16 15 14 13

This book is dedicated to the memory of two great men: Dr. Harold Paul and Coach John Wooden. Both were men of learning and leadership. They mentored me and gave me a lifelong appreciation of poetry.

HOLD ON TO YOUR DREAMS
by JIM STOVALL

*H*old on to your dreams and stand tall,

*Even when those around you would force you
to crawl.*

Hold on to your dreams as a race you must run

*Even when reality whispers, "You'll never
be done."*

*Hold on to your dreams and wait for the
miracles to come,*

Because on that miraculous day,

*Your dreams and your reality will merge
into one.*

CONTENTS

Chapter One

DISCOVERING THE TREASURE

Sometimes people, places, things, and life itself hold hidden treasures and blessings that are not apparent at first glance or, maybe, for many years to come. We deal with packaging, facades, and veneers as we stumble through this life judging every book by its cover.

As a blind person myself, I store visual images in a memory vault within my mind. I remember, as a 10-year-old, before losing my sight, my fifth-grade class got to go and visit an art museum. Like most 10-year-old boys, I had very little interest in art, but they took us to a small theatre within the museum and showed us a film about a painting being restored.

I remember the scene unfolding on the movie screen as a white-coated technician placed a painting of a clown on the workbench in front of him. The clown seemed ordinary and unremarkable. The painting was something you would imagine a high school or college student might produce.

Then, the technician began gently rubbing the painting with a white cloth he had dipped into a clear solution. Slowly, the clown began to disappear, and a fabulous landscape masterpiece emerged. Then they took us down the hall into the art gallery and showed us that masterpiece landscape fully restored.

I remember looking at that glorious painting, and I can still see it in my mind as I dictate these words. I felt as if I knew that artist and understood his thoughts and feelings. That 200-year-old French master's impression of a springtime landscape connected with me in a way no other painting ever did. The masterpiece had been discovered in a garage sale and had been hidden behind the painting of the clown for many decades.

Joye Kanelakos came into my life in much the same way. I never met her in person nor did I or anyone else comprehend the masterpieces inside of her until after she had passed away.

Joye Kanelakos was born in Pawnee, Oklahoma in 1915. She married at age 23 and raised three children. By all accounts, she was a good wife and mother. She held several nondescript, clerical and office jobs throughout her lifetime. Later in her life, her husband suffered a debilitating stroke, and Joye remained by his side as his nurse, companion, and caretaker until she passed away at age 83.

I only knew of Joye while she was living as the mother of one of my colleagues and coworkers. Joye's daughter, Dorothy Thompson, types and edits all of my weekly syndicated columns, the screenplays for my movies, and each of my books including the one you are reading right now. Through Dorothy, I sent several notes and autographed copies of my books to Joye, and she reciprocated by having Dorothy bring homemade baklava back to me. This was much more than a fair trade from my perspective.

Dorothy took some time off when her mother was hospitalized, and at a point when her death was imminent, Joye told her daughter Dorothy about a special box at the house. After Joye passed away, Dorothy and her siblings had the opportunity to go through that box, and they discovered an incomparable creative treasure. The box was filled with Joye Kanelakos's life's work as an amazing poet.

Imagine the experience of burying your mother and holding close all of the thoughts and memories of this special person you thought you knew completely, but then you discover a treasure chest of poetry like this:

> *The world awaits as morning breaks*
> *Above the rim of a shimmering hill;*
> *Color showers the skies awake,*
> *And the trees stand restless and still.*
> *Silence reigns with a gentle hand*
> *As life, still cradled in its hold,*
> *Stretches to greet the waking land*
> *All sprinkled now with silver and gold.*

Joye's poem carries my memory back over 40 years to that landscape painting by the French master in the art museum. As a blind person now for over a quarter of a century, I have to accept the fact that my visual images and the memories I carry with me of my life as a sighted person have dimmed and faded.

When Dorothy first discovered the box of poetry representing her mother's heretofore unknown creative life's work, she read the poem above to me, and that French landscape masterpiece came back into my memory, brightly lit and fully in focus. It was as if the masterpiece that the technician had revealed when he removed the clown and restored the painting had been uncovered and revealed again on the canvas of my mind through Joye's poetry.

DISCOVERY: People and things in this world are rarely as they first appear. We must be willing to dig down to the treasure beneath, and then dig deeper still to reveal the masterpiece inside of other people and ourselves.

Chapter Two

DISCOVERING THE GIFT

Each of us have special gifts. Some are more apparent than others.

If you ever heard Luciano Pavarotti or Frank Sinatra sing; watched Tom Hanks or Meryl Streep perform; or enjoyed Michael Jordan, Albert Pujols, or Brett Favre displaying their talents, it is obvious where their gifts lie.

I began losing my sight at age 17, and by age 29 I was totally blind. I had never met a blind person at that time, and I had no clue what I was going to do with the rest of my life. The only plan I could come up with at that point involved moving into this little 9- by 12-foot room in the back of my house.

In my little room, I gathered my radio, telephone, and tape recorder, and that little space became my whole world. The thought at that time of me running a major company, writing books, making movies, speaking to millions of people around the world in arena events, or even dictating these words that you are reading seemed as foreign to me then as going to the moon.

Before losing my sight, that small room in the back of my house had been where we kept our TV, VCR, and my collection of classic movies. I had always been a big fan of Humphrey Bogart, Jimmy Stewart, Cary Grant, and all of the great stars of what I consider to be the Golden Age of the motion picture industry.

As a blind person, I found myself in a prison cell of my own making, surrounded by the very best motion pictures ever made. One day, out of sheer boredom, I decided to play one of those movies. My thinking was that I had seen them all so many times that just by listening I could follow along and enjoy the story.

I picked a classic Humphrey Bogart film entitled *The Big Sleep*. As the movie played, I followed the soundtrack and could remember most of what was going on in the plot. But then somebody shot somebody else, the car sped away, someone screamed, and I forgot what happened.

I said the magic words, "Somebody ought to do something about that." The next time you hear yourself say that, you just had a great idea.

That was the beginning of my company, the Narrative Television Network, that I still run a quarter of a century later. We make movies, TV shows, and educational programming accessible for the 13 million blind and visually impaired Americans and millions more around the world.

When I first launched the television network, we could not get access to first-run movies or television network shows. The only thing we could acquire were some older movies, but as I mentioned, I was a classic film buff, so this did not deter me.

If you would like to share this service with any visually impaired people you know, or if you just want to experience how it works, you can go to narrativetv.com, close your eyes, and watch a movie.

Once we had narrated the first few classic movies, we had to get some broadcast stations and cable TV networks to carry our programming. This was difficult since we only had a bunch of old black-and-white movies that everyone already had access to.

Then it occurred to me I might be able to get some of the classic film stars who appeared in our movies to do a brief interview with me. We wrote letters to all of them we could find, and over the next few years, I interviewed Jimmy Stewart, Frank Sinatra, Steve Allen, Helen Hayes, Douglas Fairbanks Jr., and every vintage film star you can imagine.

My very first interview, however, remains my favorite for a number of reasons.

Katharine Hepburn agreed to my interview request before any of the others had responded. I used the fact that she had been a guest on my show to leverage our credibility with other stars as well as the movie industry and television networks. Miss Hepburn represented a quantum leap in my business and my life.

Katharine Hepburn was quite elderly when we sat down to have our first on-camera conversation. She had just finished working on what would turn out to be one of her last movies, and she was not doing any publicity or interviews. The entertainment trade publications had just reported she had turned down invitations to be on the late-night talk shows with both Jay Leno and David Letterman, so you can imagine how I felt when she agreed to talk with me.

If you utilized a Thesaurus and looked up terms like tough, no-nonsense, intense, or larger-than-life, I'm certain you would find the words: Katharine Hepburn.

We talked about her life and career as well as people she had known and the changes in the industry. When I had run out of all the questions I had prepared, one final inquiry occurred to me, so I asked, "Miss Hepburn, what do you think you would have done for a career if you had not been an actress?"

Without hesitating and using the voice, tone, and demeanor that has inspired generations of moviegoers, she stated emphatically, "If I had not been able to earn my living as an actress, I would have had to have found another way to support my habit. I act out of an innate need to do what I do."

I relate to Miss Hepburn's feelings every time I walk onstage to make a speech at a convention or arena event. But I had never experienced anyone else expressing the passion they felt for pursuing their gift until I read a brief five-line poem written by Joye Kanelakos.

> *Yes, she must write.*
> *Gathering her hours, she spends them*
> *Like some irrepressible sprite.*
> *Turning over life's old stones*
> *And dusting memories loose.*

DISCOVERY: We must be willing to consider our gifts and talents in new ways. The meaning of life is to find our gift, and the purpose of life is to give it away.

Chapter Three

DISCOVERING LIFE AND DEATH

Before we can learn how to fully live and experience life, we've got to come face-to-face with the reality of death. Life becomes precious when we understand that it is finite.

Teenagers and young adults often fail to grasp how precious each day is because the end to their life is nowhere in sight, or at least nowhere in their sight.

I grew up in a home as my parents' third child. This does not seem remarkable until you consider that my parents' first two children died at very early ages. My brother died of a lung disorder as an infant, and my sister died of a rare form of leukemia when she was preschool age. I never knew my brother, and as I look back, I'm not sure how well I knew my sister. The family legends and lore have a tendency to get mixed in with reality, and I'm not sure how much of my sister Nancy I experienced when I was a young child and how much I simply remember being told by my parents and other older family members. I certainly remember the family photos, her toys and clothes, as well as those awkward days each year that I later learned represented my brother and sister's birthdays, anniversary of their deaths, and other momentous occasions.

No person ever lives and dies without impacting those left behind. My brother and sister's short lives impacted my family and influenced me in many ways, some I know and understand and others, I'm certain, I can't comprehend.

As an adult, a bit of success as an author, TV and movie producer, as well as a public speaker, offered me the privilege of being exposed to some elders in the business who became friends, colleagues, and mentors.

Paul Harvey was in his 90s when our paths crossed after he read one of my books. I will never forget the day he called our office and Beth who answers our phones told me excitedly, "Paul Harvey is on the phone."

The names Paul and Harvey are both fairly common, so I asked, "THE Paul Harvey?"

Beth assured me no one else sounded quite like that, and indeed, within a few seconds of picking up the phone, I heard the voice that meant news and commentary on the issues of the day to millions of Americans. He made me so comfortable that, after that first phone conversation, I asked him if he would end the call with his signature sign-off phrase. So instead of saying, "Goodbye," he concluded with, "Paul Harvey...Good day."

Mr. Harvey wrote a priceless endorsement for my next book and became a true encouragement to me. We were both born and raised in Tulsa, Oklahoma, where he became a legend, both then and now.

Just when I was beginning to understand the privilege of having a friend like Paul Harvey, I heard the terrible news that he was gone.

Shortly after that, again through one of my books, I met and began a friendship with legendary coach John Wooden. I remember, as a young boy, sitting on the sofa with my father watching Coach Wooden's UCLA basketball teams win championship after championship. They set records that stand to this day and will probably never be approached.

When Coach Wooden was 97 years old, I recorded a series of interviews with him that impacted me greatly. I have used his wisdom in a number of my books, columns, and speeches, and someday I hope to share more of Coach Wooden with the world through other projects.

We talked about life and death, and as he celebrated his 99th birthday, it seemed much less theoretical and much more inevitable. When we lost him just short of his 100th birthday, I was struck by the tragic irony of having close friends who bring wisdom and experience into your life, but those decades of success that created that same wisdom and experience are destined to snuff out the flame of their life and your relationship with them.

I thought I had a fairly good grasp on the impact of life and death from losing my siblings as infants to losing my friends and mentors as they approached a century of life, but then I learned that Joye Kanelakos, as a child of five, dealt with the tragedy of the death of her mother.

Joye learned, as we all do, that when we lose a loved one, there is a hole left in our life and we are never quite the same. She looked back on this experience decades later, capturing the experience of a five-year-old but expressing it with wisdom and perspective gained from living a full life.

> *When I was but a child of five*
> *A stranger entered at our door.*
> *His name was death.*
> *Our mother's breath he stole*
> *To bring no more.*
> *And having once this stranger met*
> *His memory never traveled far.*

DISCOVERY: We must savor each moment with the special people in our lives as we never know which moment with them will be our last.

Chapter Four

DISCOVERING LAUGHTER

There are times when life deals a hand that requires us to either laugh or cry.

Each time I step on a stage to make a speech at a convention or arena event somewhere, I realize that I am the first blind person that many people in my audience have ever experienced in person. I struggled for several years to try to find a way to make people comfortable with my disability. I tried logic, emotion, or simply ignoring the issue, and then I found the key to success, perspective, and human connection.

I discovered laughter as an antidote to depression, despair, and tragedy.

For years, I have been sharing with my audiences a true story of an encounter I had with a deaf man. At first glance, there would seem to be few things more depressing than a blind person unless it would be a blind person meeting a deaf person, but—my dear reader—I will let you decide.

Shortly after starting my company, the Narrative Television Network, I was confronted by an emotion experienced by most businesspeople and entrepreneurs. One morning, I woke up and I came to the inescapable realization that I didn't have a clue what I was doing. If you're in business and it has not occurred to you that you don't have a clue what you're doing, it's probably already occurred to your colleagues and coworkers that you don't have a clue what you're doing.

In any event, I woke up that morning and faced the fact that there was probably no one in North America less qualified to run a television network than this blind guy from Oklahoma. So I decided to hire a consultant. This should be avoided whenever possible, but I was so paranoid about my cluelessness that I flew to Los Angeles and hired two entertainment industry business consultants.

You could tell that these guys were entertainment industry business consultants because they had both the briefcases and the pony tails. This is very important in our TV industry.

Well, I paid these two gentlemen an inordinate amount of money to come to Tulsa, Oklahoma, which is, I am sure you realize, the entertainment capital of the universe. I contracted with them to go through our operation and tell us how to run this TV network we were already running quite successfully.

I should have known there was something wrong when one of these high-priced consultants asked me with a reverent tone whether it would be okay if he picked up the Emmy Award statue that I had received for our first year on national television because he had never been so close to one.

These two consultants wandered around our offices and studios for several days and annoyed everyone in the building. Then they came into my office for the report. Overpriced consultants are big on reports.

They told me that as the founder and president of this new network and as the host of our talk show, it was expected of me in the TV industry to go on the road and meet all of our station

managers. At that time, we had hundreds of stations carrying our programming, and today we have well over 1,000.

I was just a few months past emerging from my 9- by 12-foot room and only felt comfortable in my home or at the office. So I instructed my West Coast consultants to come up with an alternative plan.

Several days later, they returned to my office and excitedly presented what they called Plan B. They explained that based on my success as an Olympic weightlifting champion, author, and businessperson, they felt they could book me into arena events and convention centers across the country as a motivational speaker, and then they could invite our station managers from across the country to come and see me when I was in their area, and that way we could kill two birds with one stone. I never was totally sure why these overpriced media consultants wanted to kill birds with stones, but apparently, it was a big deal to them.

That was when I asked the question that seems to get us all in trouble in our modern, fast-paced world. I asked, "When would I have to start?"

They explained that these large arena events are booked far in advance, and I wouldn't need to do anything for at least six months. Well, I suspect your schedule is a lot like mine in that I don't know what I'm doing later today, so I'll agree to anything six months from now. So I agreed without giving it any further thought or consideration.

In what seemed like a few days or certainly no more than a few weeks, my overpriced business consultants came back to my office and told me that it was time to go make one of those speeches I had promised them I would make.

I exclaimed, "You clowns told me I had six months!"

They calmly reassured me, "Trust us…it's been a full six months."

You see, in my world, they always lie to the blind guy, and they think they get away with it. In reality, I guess they do get away with it, but I just like to remind them that I know they get away with it.

So, finally, I was resigned to the task at hand and asked, "So where are we going, and who am I speaking to?"

They responded with pride and excitement, "We have booked you into an arena in Anaheim where you will be the motivational speaker for 14,000 state government workers."

Now, if you work for the state government, or know anyone who works for the state government, or have even discovered anyone doing any work for the state government, you'll excuse my next comment, but I thought being the motivational speaker for the state government workers was something really close to raising the dead.

Well, eventually I found myself standing backstage with our vice president Kathy Harper just a few minutes before my speech was scheduled to begin. To say I was nervous would be an understatement.

I was frantically trying to remember whether it was 12 steps or 13 to the front of the stage. For a blind guy, that can be rather critical at a certain point in time. As I was standing behind the curtain trying not to have a panic attack, I could sense that someone had approached, and they were standing right next to me. As a blind person, you become very aware of things around you, and I could just tell that someone had entered my space and was a little too close for comfort.

As I was trying to sort this out in my mind, I leaned over and said to Kathy, "I'm really nervous because I've got to raise these government people from the dead, and I forgot whether the front of the stage is 12 or 13 steps, and now I think there's someone standing here."

Kathy whispered, "There's a guy standing right next to you holding a note in front of your face for you to read."

I inquired, "What does this guy's note say?"

Kathy read his note aloud. "I am deaf. Can you please help me find the front desk."

Anxious to have this awkward encounter come to a conclusion, I turned to the deaf guy and stated emphatically, "No! I'm blind, so I can't help you find anything."

I couldn't help but think that there were 14,000 people in the building, and he's got to ask *me* where the front desk is.

I turned to Kathy and asked, "So what's he doing now?"

She explained, "He's holding the note closer."

So I explained it to him even louder, but we never did get together on that thing, and somewhere here in America there's still a poor deaf man wandering around looking for the front desk, and if you run across him, I would appreciate it if you would help him out.

For reasons I have never understood, telling this true story somehow makes my audiences comfortable with my blindness and me.

I think Joye Kanelakos understood that somewhere between agony and absurdity, we find laughter.

Help is always near,

As near as we are to our inner self.

There is a "buffer" surrounding us

Of joy, laughter, acceptance

Which will separate the important

From the ridiculous.

Pray in your possible desperation

Then laugh with God.

DISCOVERY: When we don't know whether to laugh or cry, we must remember that laughter is good medicine, and the world needs our prescription.

Chapter Five

DISCOVERING SEASONS

As I travel around the world for movie publicity, speaking engagements, or business meetings, I encounter thousands of people. In each of my books, including this one, I publish my phone number so I can hear from readers who need encouragement or want to share their victories. If you want to follow in their footsteps, just dial 918-627-1000.

Among all the calls and face-to-face meetings, I am shocked and dismayed to discover how often I meet people who are engaging in a behavior I call "wishing away your life." These people lament Mondays and can't wait until Fridays. They complain about every weather condition except for that they deem to be ideal, and they find most of the year too hot, too cold, too windy, or too wet.

The perspective of a few years or decades allows us to find the majesty and miracles in every season of every year and every hour of every day. Joye captured this wisdom in several masterpieces.

THROUGH THE KITCHEN WINDOW

I saw the rain the night before.
A rain that turned to sleet.
But first, it glazed the fence some more
And everything beneath our feet.
Preserved in ice, a clinging leaf—
All branches, limbs, and twigs
the same—
And wires from poles outside our home
Through which our comforts came.
How cold the rough sleet-blanket lay
On morning now as gray as doom,
And frost had crept the window's pane
To peer inside our shivering room.

Then, silently, the sunshine flashed
A spot of light on a startling scene,
And dancing jewels of every hue
From ruby red to emerald green.
A cardinal splashed upon my view
With impudence so brash and bold
I had to laugh although I knew
His dancing feet were getting cold.

Joye also understood that the seasons of the year parallel the seasons of our life. It's easy for young people to wish they were old and for old people to wish they were young. Too often, we expect external forces to bring us contentment and happiness.

We want the season of life to bring us joy when, in reality, we have been given the joy to bring to each season of life.

AUTUMN TWILIGHT

Walking through our lives
of many seasons

Love has given us
such wondrous Springs,
And still in autumn's glow
life's joy and laughter
Toss our hearts about
on brightened wings.
We scurried from the hard, black
storms together,
But when the lightning danced
we paused to see
The glorious majesty of God
about us,
Then walked back through
the storm's dark mystery.
And when the sun arose
on sparkling daylight
We sometimes found a flower
bent in pain,
And waited till it turned
once more to find us

Then, wrapped in love,
it struggled back again.
The snowflakes blow like
thistle-down in summer,
The hills, now plushed in white
as once in green,
Tell how the seasons blend
one with the other
And gently fold our memories
in between.
And if, one day, we step
beyond some boundary,
Wondering spellbound
as we laugh and sing,
The beauty of this time
we shared will follow
As our hearts lead us through
some bright, new Spring.

A wise man who was one of my friends and mentors once shared with me the key to happiness. When he shared this wisdom with me, he was 40 years my senior. Now that he has graduated to the next phase beyond this mortal existence, and I am approaching the age he was when he imparted these words to a clueless teenager, I am only beginning to understand the depth of his statement, "We need only three things to be happy. We require something to do, someone to love, and something to look forward to."

Joye shares that instead of our constant rush to urge the hours, days, and seasons to go faster, we need only slow down and savor each moment to capture the essence of this life as the gift it was intended to be.

OCTOBER'S PROMISES

The boughs of elm and maple sway
In gentle rhythm as to play
A tempo keyed to Autumn's tune
Lest winter bring his song too soon.

Discovering Seasons

Canna blossoms splashing red
Held stately o'er their tall-leafed bed
Stand dominant, and ask no pardon
From a sleepy, fading, pink rose-garden.
Honey from a plastic feeder
Woos a tiny humming speeder
Often now, as he vigorously guards
The dwindling nectar from October yards.
Springtime dreams and summer folly
Blend into Autumn melancholy
Bitter-sweet and warm, to hold
Deep in the heart when nights are cold.
Chrysanthemums have just begun
To fling their color at a languid sun
While silvered seeds in a dry pod holds
A promise of next year's marigolds.
Dreams, come Spring, will live again
And marigolds once more will send
Their happy greetings, underlaid
By a rug of velvet grass has made.

And, little bird, could you not stay
In that warm place so far away
Where flowers, honey-dipped all year
Would, through my logic, hold you there?
But glad am I my logic erred
And once again this tiny bird
From miles and miles some call shall hear
And one day next Spring, reappear.

DISCOVERY: Every season is a gift, every day is an opportunity, and every moment is a treasure. Spend them all wisely.

Chapter Six

DISCOVERING WORK

Our jobs and careers define us within our society. When you meet a new person, after you exchange names it is likely the next question you will ask or be asked is, "What do you do?" For better or worse, the moment that question is answered, we begin pigeon-holing people, putting them into slots and categories in our mind based on what we perceive to be their income, education, and social standing, all based upon how they choose to make their living.

Work must be much more than exchanging our time and labor for someone else's money. It is an expression of who we are, what we can give the world, and even what we will leave behind.

As a speaker, I have the opportunity to address numerous conventions of professionals. I find that there are many high-income, high-status individuals who are miserable within their career and day-to-day work.

The great entertainer George Burns was fond of saying, "If you enjoy your job, you will never work a day in your life." I have met doctors, lawyers, and investment bankers who would much rather be carpenters, landscapers, or automobile mechanics. These depressed and discouraged people are caught up in the rat race that defines an individual based upon what they earn from their work instead of what they give to their career.

Joye wrote about pursuing our life's passion and not being among those frustrated workers living the proverbial life of quiet desperation.

I wonder if my life had been

Of some completely different vein

Would I have scaled more lofty heights

Waved more banners, flashed more lights

And pressed my head where royalty has lain?

Or what if I asked but to see

Exquisite beauty just for me

Would I have ever dared to look

Beyond the diary or the book
That held the secrets wise men left
For such as we, for such as we?

When I meet people who have committed to pursuing a profession instead of their passion, I always encourage them to follow their dreams. Invariably, they will tell me how much time and money they have invested in their current career and what it would cost them to make a major change at this point in their life. There is never a convenient time to get out of your comfort zone and make a career change, but it is never a good time to toil away the hours of your life doing something you don't enjoy.

I believe you can find people at the top levels of any profession who are succeeding financially as well as nourishing their soul through work that they love.

While it may be frightening and daunting to consider leaving the comfort of a well-established—if unfulfilling—career, Joye expresses that it is more terrifying to go through one's life without pursuing one's passion and calling.

Hidden paths,
obscured by fears,
grown over by habits of worry and negativity from
doubt,
begin to appear and invite us.
These paths are our great opportunities.
Our destinies.
Our inheritance waiting for us.
This is our "good luck" we have sought forever.

As you read these words printed on a page, I am embarrassed to admit that as the bestselling author of more than 20 books, when I could read with my eyes as you are doing now, I don't know that I ever read a whole book, cover to cover. I did the minimum that was required to get through school but nothing more.

Then, after losing my sight, I discovered the National Library for the Blind which makes thousands of books available to visually impaired people in an audio format. At the same time, I had the opportunity to work with some inventors who were developing the technology that allows audio compression so that recorded books can be played at a very high speed. For the last 20 years, thanks to these resources, I have had the opportunity and privilege of reading a book from cover-to-cover each day.

This gift of books, words, thoughts, and learning has made me a different person. Becoming a reader made it possible for me to become a writer.

Through their work in the form of the written word, I have met Ernest Hemingway, Mark Twain, F. Scott Fitzgerald, James Michener, and hundreds of the greatest wordsmiths of all time. They each made a living through their work, but their books have become a legacy enjoyed by me and millions of others.

If we are to live as we were intended to, our work is more than a means to make a living or even to create a life. It becomes our lasting legacy.

OUR LEGACIES

Every footprint that we take
Makes a change where we have passed.

Small things there beneath our heel
Are changing where the print was cast.
What then could any difference make
When ruthless paths our courses take?
Beneath our heel some things will bend
Without the strength to rise again.

DISCOVERY: We must all find a way to make our career a pursuit of our passion and a means to our lasting legacy.

Chapter Seven

DISCOVERING MONEY

Money is among the most misunderstood topics in the world today. Warren Buffett is fond of saying, "People know the cost of everything and the value of nothing."

I began my professional career decades ago as an investment broker and advisor for a New York Stock Exchange member firm. When you deal with people's money, you come to understand them in different and unique ways. Money does not define our worth, but what we're willing to trade to get money may.

Through my books and movies, including *The Ultimate Gift, Financial Crossroads, The Ultimate Financial Plan, The Millionaire Map*, and others, I have come to be known as somewhat of an expert in the field of money, economics, and finance.

I have the privilege today of being invited to speak at family reunions of high-net-worth individuals. These millionaire and billionaire patriarchs and matriarchs want to be sure that the money they have invested their lives to earn doesn't ruin the second and third generations of their families.

In my book *The Ultimate Gift* and the subsequent movie based on that novel, I created a story dealing with what I felt to be life's most important lessons. I made the main character in *The Ultimate Gift* a billionaire. Not because I wanted to deal with finances in the story but because I wanted to dispel what I call "The Big Lie."

"The Big Lie" would tell us that if we just had enough money, everything in our life would be perfect. Nothing could be further from the truth. As we are trying to work harder, to earn more, to get the things we think we want out of this life, and buy the things money can buy, it's imperative that we don't lose or fail to experience the things that money can't buy.

I believe Joye was thinking these thoughts as she wrote this poem.

TODAY

Remember,
God this day unfurled
To everyone
Throughout the world.
Unblemished day,
Bejeweled and pearled—
A gift to you and me.
For each man's a tower
Or just a stone.
Born to climb higher
Or be left alone.
Time is the gift.
Use it with care.
Climb to the heights—
Our dreams flourish there.

In four short lines of verse, Joye points out one of the great human quandaries of this life. We can manage our money, our exercise, our weight, our households, and our estate, but we can never quite seem to manage ourselves.

> *I stopped for food*
> *With the wage I got.*
> *The pounds have stayed,*
> *But the money has not.*

It is important that we keep money in its proper perspective. Nothing can take the place of money in the things money does. If we go to the grocery store, our best intentions, lofty thoughts, or greatest wisdom will not complete the exchange at the checkout aisle.

Money is a reality of our lives and of our family's lives. I always encourage people of wealth to not pass along their valuables until they have passed along their values.

It's acceptable and even desirable to have long-term financial goals and objectives, but we should never get caught up in what I call "The Disease of More." If we race through our lives just accumulating more things and money for the sake of accumulating, we do not have our possessions but, instead, our possessions have us. If we can learn this when we are young and share it with our children, money takes its appropriate place in the priorities of our lives.

CHILD DICHOTOMY

My Grandma writes
Such funny stuff
About the things
I need to see—
A certain star,
A bird, or tree
Or sometimes
All about just me!
I guess she knows
The things I'll do.
She writes of schools
And double rings,
The happiness
That it will bring

When I am rich
As everything.
But Mother warns
Of too much wealth
Explained in ways
That's plain to see.
And certainly that's
Fine with me
If only half
That rich I'll be.

There is a very poignant and thought-provoking TV commercial that has received a lot of airplay. Even though I own a television network, sometimes I believe the commercials may be the best thing on TV.

In this particular ad, a young boy is leaving a voicemail message for his father who has missed his son's third-grade play in which the young boy had his acting debut. As the father played back his voicemail, he heard a beep followed by his young son's voice.

"Dad, I'm sorry you missed my school play today. I was great! Maybe you can be there next time I'm in the third grade."

Money is an infinite commodity. We can lose it and earn more later. But the passing hours and days of our lives can never be recaptured. We must balance the practical things in this world with the knowledge that we will never pass this way again, and there are sights to be seen and roses to be smelled.

SURPRISES

Beyond the reflections
Cast on the cold ground,
Past long tree-boned shadows
This morning, I found
A field of white velvet—
Snow white, and abound
With diamonds the bright sun
Had sprinkled around.
I ran for a vessel

To gather my gain.
A fortune to cushion
All want and all pain.
But when I returned there,
I sought it in vain
For the warm sun had stolen
My jewels back again.

DISCOVERY: We must always remember that money makes a great servant and a terrible master.

Chapter Eight

DISCOVERING FRIENDS

The term *friend* can be among the most significant or inconsequential words in our collective vocabulary. People have a tendency to identify every person they know or are even casually acquainted with as their friend. Facebook and the growing online digital worldwide presence has diluted the word friend even further.

We are truly blessed if we can go through a long life and count our real friends on the fingers of both hands. Friends are not simply individuals who make us feel good or bring us what we want. Friends are those people who complete us and make the road on which we travel not necessarily easier but more significant in lasting ways.

The Ultimate Gift curriculum based on my book is taught in hundreds of schools nationwide. Each semester, I go to a local university where—through technology I don't begin to understand—I am hooked up in an interactive video teleconference with hundreds of kids in their classrooms in schools across the country. These young people ask me a myriad of questions about my books, movies, and the things I believe to be true in this world.

One line of inquiry high on the list of priorities among young people is how to get others to be your friends. This question points out a generally-accepted myth in our society that friends are something we are entitled to, so we just get to have them. I believe in order to have a friend you must first be willing to be a friend. This is not always easy.

Joye's poem mirrors the old adage, "A friend in need is a friend, indeed."

This offering is particularly meaningful to me because it's one of the poems that was discovered in Joye's treasure box after her death. She wrote it as you will read it below, but it was not completed as the final line was missing. In an act of friendship toward a special lady I never met, I completed this poem.

If the poem is as significant to you as it is to me, the credit goes to Joye, and if you find it lacking, I will accept the responsibility. This is the least I can do for a friend.

LET ME BE THY SERVANT, LORD

I saw pain on faces, Lord
So plain I could detect—
Eyes that once were filled with love
Now no love can reflect.
And mirrored in the faces, Lord,
Of children at their side
The same lost look where love and hope
And expectations died.
Let me be thy servant, Lord.
Let me not walk on by
Without the words that you would say
To calm the human cry.

We are fortunate, indeed, when the people who know us best love us most.

Old friends are the best friends. Friendships are forged from common experience more than common interests. Some of my best friends disagree with me on issues including politics, faith, priorities, and some of the most important concepts in our lives. Friends do not always share our beliefs, but they find a way to both challenge and respect our beliefs.

An old and significant friendship becomes comfortable. Good friends don't have to say or do anything. They are content to just be together and be friends.

These friendships do not even require you both to be in the same place at the same time. You may not have been in the same room with a great friend for years, but they are never far from you; and when you need them to sort out a painful problem or share a cherished memory, they are always there in spirit if not in person.

Joye captured this complexity and simplicity in one thought, delivered in three lines.

Good-natured friends
are the richness
of old age.

It's easy to fall into the belief that we want to share fun, interesting, and significant experiences with our friends, but in reality, our friends make every-day experiences fun, interesting, and significant.

If you will think of the best trip or vacation you ever enjoyed, it is likely memorable, not because of where you went or what you did, but because of who accompanied you on the journey. I would rather go to a laundromat or clean out the garage with a friend than travel to the greatest places on earth with someone who doesn't challenge my mind and feed my spirit.

THE HEART OF A FRIEND

I searched life for song,
To ease life along
But my heart and song

Wouldn't blend.

Till my melody.

Took a harmony,

I heard in the voice of a friend.

I searched life for fame

And worldly acclaim

But I bought the pleasures

They lend.

Till the faith and pride,

All the world denied,

I caught in the eyes of a friend.

Life's envied treasures

We often seek first

Trade souls for bubbles

That drift on and burst.

I searched life for gold

For riches to hold

Till I came to my rainbow's end.

Then the wealth I found there,

And the blessings I share,
I found in the heart of a friend.

DISCOVERY: We become rich in this life when we calculate our wealth, not based on the money we have, but instead, the friendships we hold.

Chapter Nine

DISCOVERING PROBLEMS

Among all of the concepts I have shared in previous books, movies, columns, and my speeches, the most misunderstood idea I have ever presented is the benefit or advantage of problems.

Problems that do not defeat us serve to define us. If you will look back and consider all of the events in your life and the blessings you enjoy today, you will find that some of the best results came out of some of the worst beginnings. That feeling of chaos takes on an element of divine order when viewed through the perspective of time.

Unbeknownst to her family and friends for many decades, Joye had an abusive, traumatic, brief marriage very early in her life. She wrote about it many years later, and while the pain and anguish are still evident in her words, like all of us, Joye's problems shaped who she became and enabled her to enjoy a great marriage, a great family, and a great life in the future.

THE KNIFE

Your cold words came down all about me
And they tore out my heart with the pain
And it cried as it lay down before you
and died.
Please God—this can't happen again.
But you stood there aloof and unyielding
With a hint of a smile on your face
And I looked at this person, this creature, this
thing,
The stranger who stands in your place.
I looked on your crystalline beauty
So flawless, so icy and cold
And your pale, empty eyes made my
soul realize
You are something that love could not hold.
For the love that I offer is useless.
Tho near, never touching your heart;

As well now I see that the feeling in me
Was a dream I had built from the start.
A dream as unreal as your beauty
For they both hid the danger from me
Till I saw truth that day, turned around,
walked away
As the sharp knife of pain cut me free.

One can imagine after escaping from an abusive relationship that while the immediate threat is gone, the feelings remain. We can forgive, but often, we cannot forget. This is a struggle that we all deal with.

It is hard enough to get to the mountaintop without carrying a load of life's garbage on our backs. Somehow we have to find a way to lay our burdens down while keeping the wisdom born out of the pain and anguish with us.

HEARTS

We sing of a heart full of laughter,
We tell of a heart that is free,

We know of the broken heart after
Someone does what you did to me.
I know I can capably handle
The future since we are apart,
But I haven't a clue nor an angle
Of how I'm to manage my heart.

All of us hear two voices inside of our mind as we think about our high calling and the dreams and aspirations we have for our lives. When we think of all the things we would like to be, do, and have and how we might make a difference in this world, one voice tells us, "You have discovered your calling, and that is the purpose for which you were made." The other voice tells us, "Remember all the mistakes you made and the times you messed up. What makes you think you could ever do anything extraordinary?"

We stand at the crossroads, and our future hangs in the balance, depending upon which of the voices we listen to.

Winds of the past
That swirl and drive

Discovering Problems

You bring back a dream
That could never survive.
You wring a heart dry
Just starting to mend.
Winds of the past
Let it end.

In the following poem, Joye uses the word *tender* both to describe someone who cares for or tends to another as well as utilizing the word *tender* as an adjective for something fragile or extremely sensitive.

Problems and pain become manageable, survivable, and overcomeable when we share them, one with another. Somehow, when we share part of our burden with someone else and accept part of theirs, the load is lightened for everyone.

Child Tender—a child, tender,
Is left in your care.
His clothes were changed twice
There's still mud in his hair.

He's a small, angry angel

Who has just fallen there

And Child Tender, he feels so alone.

Heart Tender—a heart, tender,

And too small to hide

The hurried-up turmoil

That is boiling inside

Might welcome your heart

But please open it wide

Heart tender, he feels all alone.

Hurt Tender—a hurt, tender,

Could sure use the balm

Of a close, willing shoulder

And your arms to calm

The small ruffled feathers.

His tears have begun

And Hurt Tender, he thinks he's alone.

I think that we remain young as long as we believe and live as if the best days are yet to come.

We become old when we assume and live as if all of the good times are behind us.

Growing old is a state of mind and not a mathematical calculation; however, I will admit that, as the years roll by, there are more challenges to face but more wisdom and memories to lift our spirit and restore our soul.

ONE OLD BITTER DAY

I swore I'd never be this thing,

This place, this what it was they told—

I vowed I'd never reach this now

This how I am, now that I'm old!

I vowed to never feel this cringe

This back away, this care no more;

I'd cling to life, enjoy the binge,

Stay in the swim, albeit, slower.

But now I'm gripped in what's the point.

Let dangling ends continue loose.

All blanks the mind, all aches the joint

All brings the shrug of what's the use.

The rainbow bright and golden days

Don't penetrate my slovenly slot.

To share, I'd need to change my ways,

But then, who cares a heckuva lot!

We always live up to the expectations we have of ourselves or those expectations that we allow other people to place upon us. We must remember to not major in minor things.

When I was young, a wise pastor and mentor advised me, "Don't sweat the small stuff." Several years later when I had the capacity to better understand and was struggling to balance priorities in my life, he added additional wisdom by offering, "And remember, it's all small stuff."

OK - so I'm wrong.

Are there fines I should pay?

When I come on too strong?

Pass the wrong time along?

It can happen that way -

So I'm wrong.

Guess I must have forgot.

Of course, Earth failed to turn

Deserts flooded a lot

As the Arctic got hot

And the moon had to burn,

But I still forgot.

I'm sorry I'm late.

You say the meal's spoiled?

As Canada eroded

Asia Minor exploded

And the president's enemies have been foiled?

Because I was late?

That's great!

I have had the privilege of having 20 previous books published in two dozen languages with millions of copies in print all around the world; but most of the people who have read my books, watched the movies, heard me speak, or followed my weekly columns live in what we call The First World.

My late, great friend and mentor, Paul Harvey, was fond of saying, "It's not one world that we live in." He utilized this phrase before he shared a news story about The Third World countries and the people that live there.

While you and I may worry about losing a parking space, missing a sale item, or finding our lost keys, there are billions of our brothers and sisters who deal with issues of disease, hunger, and hopelessness. The next time you find yourself elevating a molehill into a mountain, ask yourself, "Is this a First World problem or a Third World problem?"

OUT OF AFRICA

And the song the boy he sang
From the heart and soul
of his tortured land
From the voiceless millions
Who prayed along

For life to stay
One more dawn.
And their song the boy he sings
It's a hopeless song
of hope that he brings.
No more can he offer
No more can he give
But his young voice demanding
They live.

DISCOVERY: Problems should not be avoided but embraced and overcome. They give us an opportunity to grow bigger and help those around us.

Chapter Ten

DISCOVERING LEARNING

Learning is a lifelong, never-ending pursuit. The great paradox exists that the more you know, the more you realize you don't know.

Several years ago, I wrote a fairy tale set in the Middle Ages in the form of a novel entitled *The Wisdom of the Ages*, and it was later released as *The King's Legacy*. In this story, a beloved and benevolent king sets out to create a lasting legacy or tribute to his reign as the ruler of the kingdom. He rejects monuments, statues, and coins bearing his image in favor of the concept of discovering and revealing the true and lasting wisdom of the ages.

He sought the wisdom of scholars, travelers, soldiers, craftsmen, and every possible individual from every walk of life throughout the land. Without revealing the culmination of the fable, it was determined that the only lasting and true wisdom of significance is held in the phrase, "Always seek wisdom."

This often comes to us when we're young but is only revealed to us in its fullness when we grow old.

WAITING

The aged, as a little child,

Before Thee, Lord, assemble

Helpless, weak, so like the child

Before Thee, Lord, we tremble.

Following the childhood days

When life exploded into youth

There was no time to merely taste

The cup life held. We grasped in haste

And gulped it all as truth.

Often, we are afraid to admit our mistakes and share them with others in fear they may think less of us. Ironically, our best lessons come from our own mistakes and, therefore, sharing the shortcomings in our own life may be our opportunity to pass along the greatest wisdom we have gained.

Never take advice from anyone who hasn't been where you want to go. We live in a world that, when it's all said and done, there's a great deal said and very little done.

My grandfather told me that "A man with experience never has to take a backseat to a man with a theory." There is no shortcut to anywhere worth going, but if you want to accelerate your success, you need to surround yourself with mentors who have been where you are and now are where you want to be.

When you communicate with mentors, elders, and those with life experience, avoid asking what they think or what they do now. Instead, ask them what they thought and what they did when they were starting their journey. Encourage them to share their mistakes and the pitfalls they experienced.

Some people never learn. Others learn from their own painful mistakes. And a few extraordinary wise souls learn from the mistakes of others.

We searched for paths the saints had trod.

In harmony, we spoke to God.

Though voice and tone were far from good—

He understood

My deepest secrets no one knew—

Till I told you.

As a writer, Joye experienced what we all who put pen to paper discover in that momentary inspiration that exhilarates us immediately does not always stand the test of time.

Sometimes, at first glance, new information or knowledge can seem dramatic and life-changing until a bit of perspective puts it in its right place.

OVERKILL

As brightly as the morning sun

Ideas began to rise,

And I jotted every lovely line

That formed before my eyes.

The idea grew so rapidly

And filled itself so beautifully
It was so richly fattened there
And plumped to near perfection.
And then I set it proudly down
Later to be groomed and honed
But when I finished, I cried to find
The poor thing trimmed and butchered
and boned.

Some people who have perfect sight somehow overlook grandeur because it seems obvious while others see the majesty in what I would call every day, commonplace miracles.

I believe among all the traits one would want in order to live an excellent life, the ability to remain curious and filled with wonderment would rank high on the list.

Sight is precious, but vision is priceless. Somehow in the process of losing my own sight, I captured a vision of who I could be. Sight tells us where we are and what's around us, but vision reveals where we could be and what is possible.

Joye shares some powerful sights but some even deeper and more powerful visions.

CALENDAR PICTURES

The true search for beauty
Requires that we look—
Dawn's beaded cobweb,
Liquid flame in a brook.
Above the lush, verdant valley floor
Granite looms up cold and bare.
Still eagles as they dip and soar
See tiny flowers, still blooming there.

Knowledge is a collection of facts, figures, and universally-accepted truths. They mean little or nothing unless you want to win trivia contests or teach facts to other people. It is better to have knowledge than not to have knowledge, but in and of itself, possessing a fact does not enable one to utilize that information in the real world.

Wisdom is an orderly collection of real-life experiences that allow us to determine how to proceed based on what we know. You've often heard it said, maybe by yourself, "I wish I had known then what I know now." This phrase is generally uttered after one suffers a painful experience. Unfortunately, the knowledge of the painful experience is what gives us wisdom to avoid that particular circumstance in the future.

We must always be careful what we are allowing our children to learn from us. The lesson isn't always what we think it is.

"Why did you do that?!" Why can't
he answer?
"What's wrong with you?" What can
he say?
"You're deliberately trying to drive us
all crazy!"
The drive he is under is often called Play.
A young mind can only hold a
small measure,
Anything over is just spilled away.
Impressions and words will become

priceless treasure,
Or he'll value rubbish, if he's led that way.

DISCOVERY: Learning is never done. Each peak of wisdom and knowledge reveals great vistas of possibility in the distance. As truth is revealed, it exposes more questions waiting to be answered.

A photo of Joye Kanelakos in a covered wagon. Joye is the baby in white being held by her older sister in the covered wagon.

Joye Kanelakos as a little girl with her mother (shortly before her mother died.)

Joye Kanelakos'
graduation photo.

Newlyweds Sam and Joye
Kanelakos in the 1930s.

Christmas at Joye Kanelakos' home.

An Easter photo from around 1949 of Sam and Joye Kanelakos with their children Steven, Mary, and Dorothy (seated on the ground).

Sam and Joye Kanelakos

Chapter Eleven

DISCOVERING FAMILY

Our families help to make us what we are just as we help to define and shape our families. They can create the backdrop of our lives and define what we believe to be normal, and then sometimes, they can create a turning point to help us move in new and better directions.

When the best medical minds we could consult collectively determined and shared the diagnosis that I was going to lose my sight, I remember the feeling of loss and disconnection from all my hopes and dreams. Then, there was the day that my grandmother came to me and explained that she had made a decision that once her spring flowers had bloomed again and she had a chance to look at them for the last time, she and I would go to one of the specialists at one of the hospitals, and she would have them take out her eyes and give them to me.

My grandmother had no way of knowing that, medically, that was impossible; but even if it had been feasible, it would have not meant as much to me to have her eyes as it meant at that moment to know that I had someone in my life that cared that much about me.

Joye shares a view of her two granddaughters climbing in the redbud trees in her back yard.

Looking out my kitchen window
What do you suppose I see?
If I think hard, I can remember
Roses climbing in my red-bud tree.

One is a rose in sunshine bloom
With two dew drops of sparkling blue,
Lips pink-tipped like the talisman
That smiles and lets the sunshine through.

The other rose is a velvet flame
And glows in smiles as warm as light
That twinkles on in her evening hair
Like dazzling sparklers in the night.

Our families are the measuring stick by which we judge the rest of the world. The concept of a "normal" family does not exist.

I have always been committed to making as many of my books as possible available as audio books. I'm a huge fan of audio books as they have changed my life. The esteemed actor, Tom Bosley, of *Happy Days* and *Father Dowling* fame honored me when he agreed to be the voice on the audio book of my novel *The Ultimate Gift*.

The year after he recorded that amazing rendition of my book, he was touring the country in the Broadway play *On Golden Pond* costarring with Michael Learned who generations will know as Olivia Walton, the mother on the classic television series.

When the show came to my hometown, Tom Bosley and Michael Learned came to meet with me in my office, and I also spent some time with them backstage after the performance. We had many discussions of their lives and careers, but then I laughingly told them, "You two have probably done more to confuse generations of people who are in search of the elusive normal family."

They both agreed with me and admitted neither of their own families looked anything like the Cunninghams or the Waltons. Families are precious and beautiful, but they are never perfect. They create the routine and heartbeat of our lives.

I wish I could have slept some more.
School is going to be a bore.
The breakfast stuff I always hate.
I have to eat or I'll be late—
My sister didn't wait for me.
She said that's how it's going to be
If I don't get myself downstairs—
But I just think nobody cares.
Wish my dad had stayed awhile.
He kissed me but I wouldn't smile.
He said he loved me anyway
And hoped I would be good today.

Our families share and help us fully experience many of life's rights of passage. There's the first step taken, the first word uttered, and—of course—the first day of school.

> *From God he came, as pure as Gold*
> *When first I gave him birth.*
> *No treasure of my fondest dreams*
> *Could measure near his worth—*
> *Then slowly my hands held him forth.*
> *I watched him run away.*
> *Then to his teacher's care, my child*
> *Became a boy that day.*

Whether it's a trip to the zoo, going to the circus, or simply experiencing the passage of time through the changing seasons, the older generations of our families help us understand the world around us while the younger generations help us to view miracles we had forgotten through new eyes.

FOUR SEASONS

Hair flowing high, face turned to the sky
Toward impatient winds that bring

DISCOVERING *Joye*

A heady aroma while earth awakes
And a stir touches everything.
My granddaughter radiantly turns to me
Saying, "Could Heaven be more near
Than when Earth is ready to burst into bloom—
Isn't Spring the best season all year?"
Memories awoke from the past as I say:
"It's the very best season, my dear."
Stopping a moment to catch up her child
And snuggle it close to her breast
Before once more it would wiggle away
Running back to the play it had left,
My lovely daughter, her face as aglow
As the ripened fruit that grew,
Said, "Mother of all the seasons you know
Which is the most perfect to you?"
Then a love for this fullness of life replied:
"Dear, I've always loved Summer best, too."
He enters the gate and smiles at the scene
Of a daughter half-child and half-grown

And a wing back and nose guard
Who plow at his back yard
With feet bigger yet than his own.
He walks to my side
And his arms sweep wide
Toward the brilliance of autumn aglow.
"It's by far the most lovely of all."
"There never will be something better
for me
Than to know I have done the job well;
The races I've run and the battles
I've won
Unashamed of what records may tell.
With a family and home that I know
are secure
I am thankful for that most of all
Mother and Dad, I'm so glad that
you're here
For my favorite season, the fall."

Each spring, I travel to my own family reunion where we all can revel in the memories and the history of the generations that have gone before while celebrating the expectation and contemplating the promise of the generations following behind.

I walk the road my fathers walked,
And feel the shade my elders knew
Cast from a sun the old moon stalked
Then overtook its shadowed view.
The same sun shone on yonder field
As horse and plow turned the soil
And pastures sprang to life anew
Where wildflowers bloomed but knew no toil.
Here a tiny brooklet flowed
Dancing, singing pebble teased.
Clear as crystal, nectar sweet
With which the very Gods were pleased.
The height of the soul from a
bare-backed mare
Neck-guided with a gentle bough

In search of wild fruit, the birds to share,
Lifts a child nearer heaven's door.

When we become adults, we are no longer children, but we can remain childlike as we share the wonder, magic, and miracles of the world around us with a child.

FAIRIES AND OTHER GOOD STUFF

When everyone is out of sight,
Or sound asleep, I stay at night
And think about some special tot,
Remembering things we liked a lot.
And in my thoughts again we're found
Out on the porch swing or uptown
Where at the park, through nook
and cranny,
You lead a huffing-puffity Granny!
Some busy folks don't understand
About the good things right at hand

To please a child to sight or touch –
And please a Grandma twice as much.
They're funny when they make a fuss
And call our best fun ludicrous
(Ludicrous means strange, you see,
Which can't apply to you and me!)
For we are serious when we think
Of Penny Peacock, a fire-blink,
Or Rosie Rabbit's powers to keep
The children safe in a forest deep.
They shouldn't scoff for we are sure
That fairies are and always were,
(A few of us, if the time we took,
Could show them where, if they'd
really look!)
In the evening late when the sun is set
And all the dark has not come yet,
While grass is warm before the dew,
There's a fairy place I've shown to you,
Where little fire-flies wink and blink –

You think they're here and then
they wink
Away off in another place,
Or sometimes right up in your face!
Then in a circle, sparkling bright
Fairy wings light up the night,
They turn and swirl and fly so free
In a rainbow dance for you and me!
On tiny, silky wings they glide
First all alone, then side by side
Around the fairy-queen, who'll swish
A magic wand for a rainbow wish.
It's sad that some folks never see
The beauty shown to you and me
So we'll just soak it up and then
Shine it back out all over them!!

I always like to encourage people to make the pilgrimage back to the family home where their ancestors lived. It offers a perspective of both time and place. If the homestead is no longer standing, a stroll through a cemetery or an afternoon with a family photo album can offer the same experience for both parent and child.

SMALL JOURNEY HOME

Stubbornly it still squats there.
Through sixty years of nature's drain
And man's neglect, the old square
Two-story shell
Determines to remain.
And now, my first and final return
Is pulling my lifetime together.
Shadows of memories
Clear as bold etchings
Will hold claim on this place forever.
From innocent days, unmarred
by pain,
Come ghosts of love that smile and then,
Reach down to softly touch my head
And we walk well-known paths again,
Before all time had fled.

Here, where tenderness abounds,
Sorrow has become unreal.
Here at last a peace is found
To help a family's youngest soul
Less loneliness to feel.

I know we are not supposed to covet that which belongs to another, and I assume this applies to writers as well; therefore, I will have to apply grace to my envy of Ernest Hemingway, F. Scott Fitzgerald, Somerset Maugham, and so many other giants including Joye Kanelakos through her poem "Children of the Wind."

In this work, Joye captures the essence of the fleeting nature of the family as the generations pull together, stretch apart, and eventually release from one another while still remaining connected in special and lasting ways.

CHILDREN OF THE WIND

Flashing in and dashing out
Gone before you're hardly seen

By ancient eyes that peer about
The emptiness where you've just been.
And often in your childish play
We heard strange names of where you stay
And live yet none here ever knew
For earthbound feet can't follow you.
But hearing, feel a longing still
When youth in innocence lays a snare
And speaks of lands beyond each hill
And tempts faint hearts to follow there.
Please stay awhile. Oh, stay with me
Sweet children of the wind
And bring what only you have seen
But cannot share again.
For in your life filled to the brim
With sights and sounds all new
I may come close, I touch the rim,
But cannot go with you.
I know you were not meant to stay
Wings young and free can never stop

But let the roar where now you soar
Rattle some ancient mountain top.
But take a part of me with you
Until once more you come again
To bring the good, the strange, the new
Sweet children of the wind.

DISCOVERY: Celebrate your family, not in spite of their imperfections but because of them. If families were perfect, they could never include people like you and me.

Chapter Twelve

DISCOVERING DREAMS

Dreams are that illusive part of each of us that at first glance could seem unreal. In actuality, our dreams have more to do with the reality of the way we live our lives in the real world than anything else.

Dreams give us the ability to go back in time and experience that which has gone before, but they also give us the opportunity to explore the miraculous empire of what can be or might be in the future.

The scriptures speak of "young men seeing visions and old men dreaming dreams." I think this speaks of what should be our lifelong quest of living our life inside out instead of outside in.

Skeptics in our world say, "I'll believe it when I see it." In reality, when you understand the power of the dream and the ability to visualize the evidence of things unseen, you'll understand that "We will see it when we believe it."

OLD DREAMS

When time becomes a golden thread

Securing memories

That otherwise might fade away

Like distant melodies

Then understand our wasted time

Is not the loss it seems.

It brings our memories back again

On webs of fragile dreams.

Our dreams not only allow us to set goals, shape our future, and pursue our calling but they allow us to get a new perspective on things that have gone before.

Events that were traumatic at the time can take on a more purposeful perspective when viewed through the lens of years or decades. Difficult people and relationships can soften and sweeten over time. The trivial can fade away as the treasure drifts to the surface.

SPRING WINDS

Flashes from old fading memories,
Dreams of love and youth long passed
Find in solitude no yearning
Feel no hurt from a wintry blast.
But in spring, abloom with laughter,
Hearts that soar on soft winds find
Lonely memories have raced after
Leaving a whimpering dream behind.

Many of the visions of our childhood or dreams of our youth fail to come to pass in the way we pictured them. For this, we can be grateful. It puts me in mind of that poignant song title and lyric, "I Thank God for Unanswered Prayer."

That which we had imagined may not materialize in quite the way we saw it in our mind's eye, but if we keep moving toward our calling with passion, we can find the reality far better than our old dreams.

AUTUMN

Like a woman
Of exquisite beauty and grace,
Fall glides across
our startled view.
Then, having passed, leaves
In her place
Discarded dreams,
For the cleaning crew.

When we were teenagers or young adults, we all had dreams, goals, and aspirations. We were convinced we were going to be the best, do the best, have the best, and change the world. Then, over time, this thing we call reality set in, and we too often find ourselves so busy making a living that we forgot to create a life.

The biggest dream you or I have ever had is still alive and well and living deep inside of us. The only thing we have to do to activate that dream is to go into that little voting booth in our soul and cast our ballot. We and our Creator are the only ones who get to vote on our dreams, and He voted for you before you were born.

When the dream's big enough, the facts don't count, and it's never too late.

Write a poem—so what if it's bad.
It's good to tell of dreams you've had.
Read a book to give your mind
A searching chance for it to find
What lies beyond.
There is so much that's there to do
Even when you're seventy-two!

DISCOVERY: Dreams are not a product of our imagination, but we are a product of our dreams.

Chapter Thirteen

DISCOVERING GIVING

Giving is among the most important and significant acts we ever perform. We think first of giving our money which is, indeed, an important part of our life. A portion of every dollar we earn or that comes to us in any way should be thoughtfully given away.

Money, however, is the least important among the gifts we should make. A portion of every day, a measure of our efforts, and a part of ourselves should be given to others.

The concept of giving introduces one of the great universal paradoxes of this life. The more you give, the more you will have. This is not to say we should give in order to get, but it simply confirms the order of life and the essence of creation.

THINK OF ME

When you, by chance, may think of me
Remember, please, some kindness
That once or twice I may have shown
When I forgot the blindness
Of prejudice or hate and spite
And showed unselfish care
And shared a day or dreamed a night
And left no hurting there.
And if some part of what is me
Some day you seek to take
And make it into what you'd be
I hope for each our sake
The part so easy to recall
So fast to come again
Will sing of spring and love for all
And leave no room for pain.

When we think about giving, we also must consider all that we have been given. Whether it's in your personal or professional life, none of us is, indeed, an island, and there have been a myriad of family, friends, coaches, mentors, teachers, and all manner of significant people who have come into our lives to pour a bit of themselves into us. When we think of them, how can we not give a part of ourselves and all that we have to others?

> *Who gives us all*
> *the joys on earth,*
> *And lights our hearts*
> *with fun and mirth*
> *Who gives her all*
> *for all she's worth?*
> *You do.*
> *Who tolerates each*
> *stupid plan*
> *Withholding snickers*
> *best you can*
> *Who pleases since*
> *She first began?*

You do.
And who, with love
so quiet & dear
Quiets us too
of things we fear
With a kind, giving word
Or a gift to hold near?
Who do?
You do!

A major factor in giving is to understand the cycle of life and death, sowing and reaping, as well as giving and receiving.

While we do most of our giving in a human sense, we need to be ever mindful of all we have been given in a spiritual and practical sense from our Creator. The eternity of life has already begun.

EARLY GIFTS

We need not wait
For death to come

Chapter Fourteen

DISCOVERING GRATITUDE

Among all of the concepts I have introduced through my books, movies, columns, and speeches, the one adopted by more people in their lives—judging from my calls, letters, email, and comments from people I meet in my travels—is The Golden List.

The Golden List is a tool I shared originally in my novel *The Ultimate Gift* and the subsequent movie. Since then, The Golden List has become a permanent fixture in a number of my books, columns, movies, and speeches. I would like to take credit for creating The Golden List, but like much of the great wisdom I have shared through my work, I have to admit to being only the delivery boy.

When I was very young, I had to spend a lot of time at my grandparents' house due to the

hospitalization or treatment of one or another of my siblings. This took me out of a home, neighborhood, and circle of friends where I was comfortable.

Apparently, I expressed my displeasure and discontent to a degree that prompted my grandmother to introduce me to The Golden List. In the midst of my ranting, raving, and complaining, she interrupted me and explained, "You can criticize, complain, and whine all you want as soon as we fill out your Golden List."

When I inquired, "What's a Golden List?", she explained to me that we simply needed to take out a sheet of paper and write down 10 things for which I was grateful and thankful. Then I could continue my complaining. Well, as I'm sure you can imagine, I never got close to the end of The Golden List before I forgot what I was complaining about.

Gratitude is not a product of celebrating getting all the things we wanted. Gratitude is a product of recognizing that we wanted all the things we got.

When Dorothy opened her mother's treasure box of poetry, she discovered that Joye and my grandmother had a lot in common.

THE SPARKLERS OF LIFE

Children (any age)

Surprises/delightful things

Softnesses

   Smiles

   Looks

   Snow scenes

   New life

Beauty

   Love

   Voices

   Understanding

   Friendship

   Quiet

   Earth

      Spring color

      Life

      Snow-softened winter.

Gratitude needs to become a lifelong pursuit and trait. We need to exercise thankfulness in every situation. Often, things that do not seem like blessings or benefits when they first arrive on the scene somehow, over time, take on a significant role among the great things in our lives.

My friend and mentor, the late, great Coach John Wooden, was fond of saying, "Things turn out best for those who make the best of the way things turn out."

Joye understood that something need not start out right or end up perfect to be something we should be grateful for.

CHOICES

The sun arose ahead of me
And tho the day was free
I took the chance to scold myself
For resting needlessly.
But looking on the lovely day
And grateful for sweet healing rest

I felt compelled to thank someone
For I felt truly blessed.
Now catching up at twice the pace
Meant racing with the clock.
I looked it squarely in the face
And matched it, tick for tock.
And once the scurried pace was set
I kept it all day long
I scrubbed and shined and tried to get
All things right I thought wrong.
But when I did decide to leave
And ran to chase the sun
My choice and time chose to deceive—
The golden day was gone.

Happiness is a choice. All of us live up to the expectations we have of ourselves or those expectations we allow other people to place upon us.

I remember being at a speaking event with my friend and colleague Zig Ziglar. We were back-stage and nothing seemed to be going right. The lights and sound were not functioning properly, the agenda was chaotic and out-of-order, and deliveries that had been expected had not arrived at the arena.

Zig, displaying his usual unflappable great attitude, declared, "Well, it's going to be a great day today!"

One of the stagehands sarcastically responded, "Well, you seem to be having a good day today."

Zig stopped, smiled, and gave one of his wise and memorable answers. "Many years ago, I decided to have a great day...today."

HOW ARE YOU?

I am as healthy as I believe myself to be.

I am as wealthy as I believe

I am only as blessed as I consider

myself blessed

I am as happy as I will allow myself

to become.

My life is as productive as I, myself, will permit.

This morning before coming into my office to dictate this chapter to Dorothy, I was listening to the radio as I was getting ready for work. The weatherman was lamenting the long-range forecast for the winter ahead. Obviously, he had not experienced Joye expressing her gratitude for a snowy day.

One morning, past, I pushed my door
And watched a fan form at my feet
Where snow lay on the front porch floor
And yards beyond, a breathless treat.
A waiting, pure white world of peace.
No sound I heard but one faint call,
Of bird, a crow, far to the east
Then silence, once more, covered all.
Into this predawn, soft surprise
This gift, unblemished, for my soul,
Hushed with quiet, patience, peace,
I stepped and let the beauty in.

Gratitude is a habit that must be developed. It is a muscle that must be exercised regularly. Ironically, the greatest blessings for which we should be most thankful are often the easiest to overlook.

THANKSGIVING

Sometimes I watch in silence, awed,
While morning splashes light
Across the sky, then paints the hills
That rise up from the night.
And gratitude is so profound
At the peace and harmony
That I must humbly ask my God:
Why was this given me?
For I can stretch and reach as free
As any bird above
Or I can roam the length and breadth
Of this sweet land I love,
Or know that I may till this soil
Or build here where I stand

And freedom lets me reap the gains
For future dreams I've planned.
And when my soul in gratitude
Bids me to go in prayer
To any shrine that I desire,
No law forbids me there.
And when I see the colors
Of our nation's flag unfurled
Over people it has gathered
From all corners of the world
I'm reminded then of blessings
That the peace of Heaven blends
In the sunrise, on the hilltops,
In the faces of my friends.

Gratitude needs to become a lifelong compo-
nent of our personality for all of us, because the
perspective of the mounting years gives us a perch
from which to better understand that which has
gone before and why we should be thankful for it.

One of my great business mentors, Lee Braxton, was fond of describing temporary business setbacks as disguised opportunities.

I can still hear him saying, "This will turn out to be one of those million dollar experiences that I wouldn't give you a nickel for today."

None of us is wise enough to be a pessimist or remain ungrateful. You may not be thankful for the plowing, planting, cultivating, and fertilizing, but just wait for the flower and rejoice.

> *In the sweet tranquility of youth*
> *When cares like red balloons will*
> *drift away,*
> *Happiness is a granted gift in space*
> *That knows no anxiety but play.*
> *And happiness is taken as a grant.*
> *These joys come back to heal*
> *another day.*

DISCOVERY: Being grateful today makes you appreciate yesterday and anticipate tomorrow.

Chapter Fifteen

DISCOVERING A DAY

I am often asked about the key to having a successful life, a successful business, or a successful career. There are, obviously, many elements that go into success.

Reaching our goals is rarely a short-term proposition. The people who win in life stay focused over a long period of time; however, if I had to identify one factor that could make any person succeed, it would be understanding the power and significance of every day.

In order to have a good life, in either personal or professional terms, you have to have a series of good years. In order to have a good year, you must have a series of good months. In order to have a good month, you must have a series of good weeks. And, therefore, in order to have a good week, you must have a series of good days, beginning today.

In a two-line offering, Joye confirms that each day is a blank canvas, neither good nor bad, until we make our mark upon it.

> *Neither sad nor happy days,*
> *Nor contented days, but my days.*

In order to make each day a success as we pursue the mission of our life, we've got to protect our attitude and our day from outside factors.

People and circumstances will invariably conspire to seemingly attempt to ruin your day. They cannot ruin your day, but they can ruin your attitude, and you can ruin your day.

> *Let not the soul,*
> *Made perfect in the image of God*
> *And endowed with his Holy Spirit,*
> *Be contaminated*
> *From the bitterness and strife we meet*
> *During the spending of this*
> *Golden Gift.*

This irreplaceably precious
Day of Life.

I am an early riser as I believe it gives me a head start on the rest of the world as well as my day. I'm a big believer in the great song lyric that assures us that morning is "the best part of the day."

NEW LIGHT

I open my eyes to you
Bright shiny morning,
While some lonely half-dream
Still clouds my mind;
And I worry your presence
By pulling in yesterday,
Plucking out moments
I should leave behind.
Sweet friend and companion,
Refresher of souls,
I rise to your joyful
Awakening at last.

And I gather your warmth
As a maiden her lover.
Embrace me, sweet morning—
Black shadows are past.

Like anything else in our lives, rainclouds and storms—be they internal or external—can only affect us in ways that we allow them to.

Joye expresses that a rainy day on the outside can give you an opportunity for reflection, introspection, and planning inside, and better yet, it can offer you an opportunity to rejoice outdoors.

PLINK PLANK

It was so dark when I arose
I didn't need to look to see
The rain remains, and I suppose
Another day is lost for me.
Sometimes, to spend a day inside
Can be the greatest thing to do.
A time to think and dream or hide
From duties somewhere calling you.

Discovering a Day

As grudgingly I settle down
And try to concentrate and think
Through dreary thoughts there comes
a sound
A dancing, happy, snappy "plink."
I've chosen the remotest place
Where there should be no noise real soon
But tiny raindrops on the flu
Plink, plank a spanking brand
new tune.
Softly, tiny gentle drops
Were bringing me their melody
Delightful and refreshing plops—
In dancing, rain-time harmony.
Each one has gone to so much pain
To leave such happy note so free.
I'm heading straight out in the rain
So they can play "Plink, plank"
with me.

My late, great friend and mentor Coach John Wooden was fond of reminding his players and those of us who had the privilege of learning from him that "You will be known for a lifetime of great things you do or a single mistake, so make each day your masterpiece."

Every moment of every day, we have the privilege of being a positive force in the world or a negative force in the world. It is impossible not to impact other people and things as we go through our daily routine, so we must determine to leave a positive impact through every word and deed in every day.

TODAY

If I keep my step
Soft this day
And monitor the words
I say
And guard each deed
Along my way—

What will this profit me?
What could one single
Day of choice
With or without
Cause to rejoice
Be it in silence
or full voice—
Would either profit me?
If angry feet
Are treading mine
And words so thoughtless
And unkind
Leave stinging pain
And hate behind—
Will this, too, profit me?
And when I take
That bruise you give
And treasure it
Wherein I live
Will it become

A worn-out sieve

And let love drain away?

For if we steal

The dignity

Of someone weaker yet

Than we

Will strength become

Infirmity?

Perhaps the scowl

My countenance shed,

The angry, hurtful

Words I said

Remained from when

My own heart bled

From others' insensitivity.

Remember, God

This day unfurled

To everyone

Throughout the world

Unblemished day,

Bejeweled and pearled—
A gift to you and me.

DISCOVERY: Some people's lives will last a century while others but a few decades, and some people's time on this earth will only be counted in terms of a few years. But in the final analysis, we all have today.

Chapter Sixteen

DISCOVERING LOVE

Love is an all-encompassing emotion and life force that defies description and even definition. In the English language, the word *love* is used universally. It has been expanded to mean virtually everything and, therefore, means virtually nothing.

I may love my dog, hamburgers, my mother, the St. Louis Cardinals, my wife, autumn, and old friends. When you love someone or something else, the depth of the feeling and the height of the emotion is fully known only to you.

Love does not require another to be perfect. It requires them only to be fully themselves. We only can give love freely and not conditionally. We must love others for who they have been, who they are, and who we hope they can be.

Look into the depths
Of another's soul
And listen,
Not only with our ears,
But with our hearts,
And imagination,
And our silent love.

In this life, we don't always get what we want, need, or deserve, but we always get what we expect. Too many people are looking for love from others. We can only give it away and wait for it to come to us expectantly.

I awoke this morning
With a prayer of gratefulness;
A prayer of hopefulness
And joy.
To a God of love—
I asked for Love—

A house filled with it.

I seek and expect a home

Bursting its seams and lifting the roof

with Love,

Driving out everything else

And making a place for angels to enter

And sing of the promise:

"Where love is, there I am also."

Some of the deepest questions of the human condition were put into words and presented to us by literary masters. The essence of life and death were defined in Shakespeare's question, "To be or not to be." Lord Alfred Tennyson considered the ecstasy and agony of love when he posed the question, "Is it better to have loved and lost then never loved at all?"

Love always represents the best and highest ideals of who we are and who we were created to be. Pain will diminish, dissipate, and disappear, and only love will remain.

I LOST

I went for it all, not heeding the cost.
I only looked once before the coin tossed;
I laid down my heart—and I lost.

The best times, places, and experiences can be enhanced and embraced as we share them with those we love.

The silver light wakens
Its sweet morning time.
A gentle breeze beckons
For the sun to come shine.
I search for the morning
All bright and so new.
That's one of the times
When I think of you.

If we want to share love or any emotion with the whole world or just those around us, we must first master the universe that exists inside our heart, mind, and soul.

We can only share that which we possess and that which possesses us. To give love away, we must first accept it, then embrace it, then become it.

PEACE

My heart prayed, "Lord, what can I do
To cause world hate to cease?"
And through my thoughts there came
to me
The soft words: "Peace, bring Peace."
Can one so spiritually immature
Know where or how to start?
Again within my thoughts I heard:
"Bring peace to your own heart."
How small a place, yet oh so great
For nothing can begin
To channel love through walls of hate
Which lets no warmth within.
For when the heart is open wide
And love is flowing through

Then can a sweet, sweet peace abide

Within each day anew.

For in God's plan there is no waste

And the peace you share with me

Does not end here, but travels on

And on eternally.

These tiny bits of healing peace

Given to us to share

May be the start that heals the heart

Of suffering everywhere.

How small a place, but oh so great

When once we do begin

To welcome God's own peace and love

And let it dwell therein.

And as it grows, it overflows

To still another place.

For love surrounds and then rebounds

In overwhelming grace.

DISCOVERY: Where love abides in its full and unconditional form, no other emotion can exist.

Chapter Seventeen

DISCOVERING HOLIDAYS

Holidays are the punctuation in our years. They are the milestones of our lives.

To paraphrase Dickens, they can be the best of times and the worst of times, but like everything else in our lives, we have the right to choose, and we change our lives when we change our minds.

I remember, during my teenaged years, visiting my grandparents each holiday season. We would take our accustomed places around the dinner table to enjoy the long-anticipated feast.

I remember the year that I came face-to-face with my looming diagnosis of blindness. As I sat at the table in my place where I had been the year before and the year before that, I realized that the antique clock across the room—which had been clearly visible several years ago and dim last year—had finally disappeared from my world. At the same time, I realized that the loved ones around me were diminishing, too, through the marching forces of age and infirmity. I realized it was only a matter of time until they disappeared from my world as well.

Then the miracle occurred to me when I realized those special times and places are memories that I can take with me. The love and feelings they elicited then are alive and well now and have made me who I am.

THE CHRISTMAS HEART

Now comes the loveliest time of year
When Heaven descends and binds so near
That even the few who scoff and poof
Have a terrible time remaining aloof.
For the Christmas heart is a happy heart
And brings to the step a snappy start.
It waves the hand, it smiles the face,
And dumps its love all over the place.
So we thrill to the joy of a

Christmas heart.
A 'Come let us share it together' heart,
A 'Please let me give, for I love you' heart
Like the beautiful heart of the Child.
One Christmas heart is a tired heart;
Big callused hands on a shopping cart
With a billfold spilled at the local mart
Like the generous heart of the Child.
For a loving heart is a living heart
An 'All that I have I am giving' heart,
A love beyond understanding heart
Like the wondrous heart of the Child.
Blest above all is the warmest heart
As the parent, child and family start
Reaching out to embrace some
unloving heart
In the all-loving name of God's Child.

I remember fondly that time each fall when we would dress up in a costume of our own making and rush around the neighborhood collecting untold quantities of treasure laden with sugar and chocolate.

No matter what character we became or form we assumed for that one evening, we learned the difference between reality and make-believe.

TREATS

Toddling goblins, frocked and masked,
Conquer the difficult steps and then
Silently wait until treats are passed
Like patient, hungry little old men.

I've always thought that somehow Thanksgiving and Christmas were out of order on the calendar. It seems to me that Thanksgiving was about being thankful for all we have, and Christmas, unfortunately, has become about getting the things we don't have. But, maybe, if we celebrate Thanksgiving enough, we will realize we have everything we want and need long before the Christmas presents are opened.

Next to Christmas, I suppose
Thanksgiving is the best.
Because it helps us realize
How richly we've been blessed.
The great expanse of beauty
Found throughout our gracious land.
The spacious gifts of woody hills
And plains the miles have spanned
And more of rich abundance
Than our sense can comprehend
Though often we won't take the time
To see what's here at hand.

As a child, I was convinced nothing was better than rushing from door-to-door and being presented with candy at each house. Much later in life, I realized that the greatest fun and most wonderful experience is that of having the energy and exuberance of countless children ringing your doorbell with great expectation.

Once again, I am reminded that giving is better than receiving.

I've always thought the tales of spooks

Were just somebody talking.

But this year, I have been convinced

There were some Gremlins walking.

We are in danger of missing the meaning, message, and miracles embodied in each of our holidays. We need to always realize that it is a celebration and not a chore.

When you strip away all the layers, the glitter, and all the tinsel, you will find that this next Christmas can be as significant as the first one.

THE SPIRIT OF CHRISTMAS TIRED

All at once, it has become

A less than happy scene.

The sparkling holiday trim is shelved,

Sacked and packed and stacked, unseen.

A busy sweeper rattles and hums

And lives on errant glittering specks

Or a few well-trampled cookie crumbs

Or smashed potato chips.

This is the Spirit of Christmas Tired,

Too much all and overdone.

Too much substitute for love.

Too much artificial fun.

Plastic wheels with honks and squawks,

Plastic dreams that fall apart.

Dreams now crushed and left to mock

Tears from an equally fragile heart.

Beyond a glassed-in window view

Asleep beneath colors of brown and gray

The back yard waits for spring to brew

An even lovelier holiday.

For seeking to soften the memory

Of the Savior's death on a barren cross

Earth will burst to a brilliant sea

For the playful breeze to tease and toss.

DISCOVERY: As you celebrate the holidays with your loved ones each year, make them all special. The holidays will always be there, but your loved ones will not.

Chapter Eighteen

DISCOVERING INSPIRATION

Inspiration is the first thing we receive as we enter this world and the last thing we leave behind as we depart. Some inspiration is shared directly with us through the Creator or the creation, but much of that which inspires us comes through others who have gone before but shared their words, deeds, and love with us.

FOR ME

Surely, somewhere in my life,
There came a moment near sublime
That we have shared, one fragile bliss—
Remember this.
Or standing at a cavernous edge
Where eons of stress had left its dredge

Then draped it o'er in beautiful hue—
Take this with you.
And should unhappiness try to stay
Shut it aside. Recall that day
We laughed 'til every hurt was gone—
Please keep this one.
For anguish I have caused, forgive,
And through life's unrelenting sieve
Pluck out some shiny bit of me
And kindly let all pain fall free—
Do this for me.

Joye shares a bit of unparalleled wisdom with us. It is our tendency to want to proclaim the thoughts we have inside of us with the world around us, but if we will only take care of the plot we have been given and accept the wisdom that is being shared with us, the world will become a better place—one person at a time.

Perhaps the answer to the dilemma
Of our world is for each of us
To keep the waters of this,

His own tiny space,
Unpolluted and tranquil.
I know God is here,
I sense his smile
As I rejoice when things work well
And when I remember to be grateful.
I feel His peace
As I become peaceful and unafraid.
It is at such times
That I feel I have sensed a flash
Of the indescribable majesty
That is God
And even I have been touched by the
awesome power
Of His love.

From the point of our earliest memories, we have been admonished to grow up, mature, and be an adult. While there are great things about maturity and adulthood, many of the better traits we seek to develop were inside of us when we were born. We need only keep out of the way and, with childlike faith, become who we were meant to be.

SUFFER THE LITTLE CHILDREN

Suffer my presence, forbid me not
As when Jesus called me near
And patiently showered his blessings
of love,
Dispelling my infantile fear.
Suffer my presence, forbid me not,
His blessings are still nearby.
For the Kingdom of Heaven and God's
purest love
Have been given to such as I.
Suffer my reaching hands to touch
The arms of benevolence
From wiser, older ones I trust
With innocent confidence.
Suffer my presence, forbidding me not
This moment, it's all that I own—

This golden moment to you I have brought

From the Master's mighty throne.

Suffer my needs and forbid them not

As Jesus would have it be

Before I am plunged into worldly rot

That will steal God's love from me.

Suffer my presence, lest man invite

And by unholy deeds convey

God's wrath unfurled in all of its might

For one Innocent led astray.

Offering and accepting forgiveness is at the core of all human yearning and the essence of our higher calling.

I sought my God expectantly

Pledging mind and soul to live

For nothing but His call for me

And all that I had vowed to give.

Through daily prayer I sought my God

To worship Him and praise His name.
I walked new paths for me untrod
But still my heart remained the same.
Until at last I bent my knee
And begged my God to take the sin
That kept my heart from soaring free
Because of binding chains within.
Then I felt someone reach and touch
Where I alone refused to go.
Forgivingly, He turned around
The hate and fear that bound me so.

Sometimes in order to hear, learn, and understand that which we seek, we need only to be still.

Only when we allow the soul
Soft and gentle thoughts to hold
Will we receive the blessings sweet
The listening silence can unfold.

Often, the best way to move forward and hold on is to simply let go.

Abide, dear Lord, while I decide
What is wise to say or do.
May I then know to step aside
And clear the path for you.

DISCOVERY: Inspiration can be found packaged between the covers of a book, within the verses of a song, or the stanzas of a poem, but it also resides in the whispering wind, a baby's laugh, and the nightly sunset.

Chapter Nineteen

DISCOVERING YOUR DESTINY

I have enjoyed this voyage of discovery with you and those around the world who will read this book. Being able to experience, savor, and share the treasure of Joye Kanelakos's poetry and artistry with the world is a distinct honor.

Though our journey together in this book is drawing to a close, great poetry is like an old friend or a fine wine that grows better with age. You can revisit this book, these chapters, and Joye's individual poems throughout the rest of your life, and share them with others in your world.

At first glance, Joye Kanelakos, like most of us, would be considered a common person. Her talent and genius were not readily apparent and did not fully come to light during her lifetime. I think it is important for you and me to understand that we all have gifts and treasures inside of us. Most people go to their graves with their song unsung, their masterpiece unpainted, and their poetry never written.

While Joye never fully understood the impact of the fruits of her labor, she had that satisfaction that every artist knows of letting the innate greatness within flourish in the light of day.

I hope you will look at your life, your calling, and your destiny in new ways, and I hope you will begin to build your own legacy that others may enjoy just as you and I have enjoyed Joye's life's work.

To help you begin crafting your own inspiration, I hope you will enjoy one of my humble efforts at poetry.

CORNERSTONES
by JIM STOVALL

If I am to dream, let me dream magnificently.
Let me dream grand and lofty thoughts
and ideals

That are worthy of me and my best efforts.
If I am to strive, let me strive mightily.
Let me spend myself and my very being
In a quest for that magnificent dream.
And, if I am to stumble, let me stumble
but persevere.
Let me learn, grow, and expand myself to join
the battle renewed –
Another day and another day and
another day.
If I am to win, as I must, let me do so with
honor, humility, and gratitude
For those people and things that have made
winning possible
And so very sweet.
For each of us has been given life as an empty
plot of ground
With four cornerstones.
These four cornerstones are the ability
to dream,

The ability to strive,

The ability to stumble but persevere,

And the ability to win.

The common man sees his plot of ground as little more

Than a place to sit and ponder the things that will never be.

But the uncommon man sees his plot of ground as a castle,

A cathedral,

A place of learning and healing.

For the uncommon man understands that in these four cornerstones

The Almighty has given us anything – and everything.

We all stand at the crossroads of greatness and mediocrity. Day by day and moment by moment, we are faced with the challenge of moving forward toward our calling, becoming stagnant in our mediocrity, or slipping backward into oblivion.

Whenever we are tempted to do anything less than light a candle and allow our beacon to shine into this world of darkness, we need to heed Joye's admonition.

RELEASE ME

The smiling, mirrored face you see
Will please the ones you greet
And I am once more tucked away
Unknown to those you'll meet.
But I am here, you've nurtured me
Within your bitter care,
I am a thought straight from your heart –
Release me, if you dare!
Released, I'm free to form a word,
Together we have grown,
Till you'll need twice the strength to fight
The foothold we have won.
For now I can move bolder still
And less restricted be,

DISCOVERING *Joye*

I am the word your thought has made –
Release me, and I'm free!
I travel now as fast as sound,
Till I'm the deed you'll try,
To all intent, we seem hell-bent
The thought, the word and I!
The deed released can then explode
Into a million parts,
Each one a tear, flung far and near
On unsuspecting hearts!

DISCOVERY: There is a master plan for each of us that includes a grand design for all the days of our lives. Once we have captured that vision of the Promised Land, anything less cannot be tolerated. As we pursue our calling, we will inevitably stand on the mountaintop and see from whence we have come, and only at that moment will we realize we have not arrived but merely reached a vantage point from which to view a more distant summit, a loftier pinnacle, and our higher calling.

ABOUT JIM STOVALL

Jim Stovall is the president of the Emmy Award-winning Narrative Television Network. He is the author of the bestselling book, *The Ultimate Gift,* which is now a major motion picture starring James Garner and Abigail Breslin. He has authored 20 other books that have been translated into over two dozen languages. He can be reached at Jim@JimStovall.com.